Making The Shift

*Activating Personal
Transformations To BECOME
What You Should Have BEEN*

Vincent K. Harris

Making The Shift

Activating Personal Transformations To BECOME What You Should Have BEEN

Vincent K. Harris

Download FREE documents and videos by visiting www.MakingTheShiftBook.com/bonus as a thank you for your purchase.

Harris, Vincent K.
Making The Shift / authored by Vincent K. Harris

ISBN-13: 978-1482047486
ISBN-10: 1482047489

Book Cover Design: Lee Enterprises, LLC

Editing Services by: Shane Grant

Initial Content Review by: His Purpose, LLC

Table of Contents

Introduction: There Is Hope

Often times, we hear of ways to prosper. We have read the tips to successfully build our dreams, been told several mantras to help motivate us, and given the steps to pursue our goals or further our careers, but not often are we taught principles to pursue our dreams and stick to them. We've heard quotes such as: "If you believe it, you can achieve it" or "If you dream it, you can obtain it." Not to say these popular sayings are not true, but there is more to it than just saying them.

Think about someone, maybe yourself, who has a wall filled with sticky notes and quotes around their home, office, cubicle, wall or mirror. We put these notes up as daily reminders of encouragement for ourselves or for others. We see them and occasionally read them but rarely meditate on them. Often times, with some people, the sticky notes or printouts become mere décor. They become a fixture, and not a passion. Sometimes they fall off, frustrations arise and because we don't speak positively, those quotes and words of encouragement are not retained. As a result, many of us never pursue our true passions. Yet, the absolute best way to create wealth is to discover your passion, perfect it and then prosper by distributing it through a system. Most people are so busy trying to make a living, yet they never learn how to make a fortune by discovering and perfecting their passion, which is a HUGE problem.

What is your passion? Your passion helps you to understand your purpose and your purpose determines your potential. People who are unaware of their passion can never know their potential or what they are capable of achieving in life. You must know your passion to understand the possibilities of your future.

Your passion is that "thing", "cause" or "calling" you have embraced and are willing to sacrifice life and all of your resources for in order to obtain or accomplish it. It's the thing that keeps you motivated, excited and enthusiastic about life even when things are challenging. Your passion speaks to you daily and even when you really want to throw in the towel, you are unable to because of the call of your passion. Your passion will not allow you to be average or settle for where you are. Instead, it calls you to fulfill the greatness erupting on the inside of you. Your passion helps you become more than what you are right now.

By no means am I insinuating that where you are right now is not a great place to be, especially if you have accomplished significant goals. But, we should all desire to reach the next level or goal. It should always lead to the ultimate level of your passion. There is always room for growth.

There are factors in determining how far you are willing to go to get to where you are destined to be. Understand this, anytime you set a goal and accomplish that goal, you should begin working on the next one. You may have an ultimate goal of owning a business, but there are several proceeding goals that need to be accomplished before you can achieve the next. My goal in this book is to help you focus while reaching to obtain your passion. Believing your dreams can be accomplished, mental toughness, and motivation are guiding principles, personal transformations if you will, that help you sustain while reaching your mark. They all work together. The system provided in this book will keep you focused and give you clarity on maintaining a winning spirit through a "date with your future" concept. These personal transformations are the premise for this book and through the explanation and illustration of each, I hope you will have a more solid foundation, keen awareness and better outlook for what can truly become active in your life. By implementing the principles outlined in this book, your world can dramatically change for better!

Each chapter represents a lesson I learned during some of the most challenging times in my life. Throughout those challenging times, I would continually pray: *"God, you are the creator of my life and I know you have a specific purpose for my life. Help me to focus on You and know the greatest reward will be the hope others tap into because of the mercy and grace You've bestowed upon my life."* This book is a portion of the challenges, solutions, and the hope He has given me to help bring deliverance and freedom to others who are broken, stuck, confused, and hurting during those challenging moments in life.

This book is divided into lessons I've learned throughout my journey in three distinct stages. First, I had to get real and face the truth about myself. Secondly, I had to go through an internal motivation. Lastly, once I was focused and strong enough, I was able to apply financial principles that are proven. Within each stage, I share the lessons learned along with potential solutions to an array of problems. Without delay, let's begin to make the shift.

Part One: Motivational Factors and Affirmations

Chapter 1
You Are More Than What You've Become

In the movie "The Lion King", Mufasa, the king, was killed trying to rescue his son, Simba, in a stampede planned by his brother Scar. After being killed, Scar convinced Simba it was his fault and told Simba to run away so he wouldn't be accused of his father's death. Now, right before this scene, Simba was excited and singing about how he couldn't wait to be "King." But one of the mistakes he made when the death of his father occurred is that he listened to his fears more than he listened to his dreams.

Throughout your entire life, you will be exposed to two different voices with two different messages. One will be very domineering and reinforced by friends, the media and the world at large. The other will be voiced by only a few and its message will be attacked by the masses. You will be forced to choose which voice or path you follow. Choose wisely because the destination of your family will be determined by the choice you make today. Let's review the two voices:

Voice #1: Fear – This voice will tell you to never try anything new and shows you over and over again in the dark room of your mind, all of the negative possibilities that could occur (Scar telling Simba he was the reason for his father's death). It will lead you to believe that if you try and fail, you are a failure and you will be embarrassed and ridiculed by the masses. This voice will cause you to be frozen in a time, a place in your life you hate, but you will grow to accept it because everyone else seems to be in the same place so it must be right.

Initially, Simba listened to his voice of fear. He left the village and started hanging out with two individuals named Timon and Pumbaa who wanted nothing out of life, and gradually, Simba lowered his standards to those around him even though he was born to be king. As a matter of position, he was king but practically he was living beneath his potential. Look at all the time Simba wasted before deciding to fulfill his purpose and destiny. Are you doing to the same?

Voice #2: Dreams – This voice will show you a life very few live if you are willing to make the necessary sacrifices. There will be struggles and obstacles; however, the passion of your dreams will propel you to success. Lives will change because you dare to be different and you inspire others with the hope for a better tomorrow. You feel freedom just by pursuing the dream and even if you don't achieve it, there will be no regrets in your life and you would have lived life to its fullest. This voice becomes the dominant voice because you learned to listen to those dreams more than your fears and teach others to do the same – and it's the only way to really obtain freedom.

Another mistake Simba made was that he did not want to become King bad enough. He left without facing the obstacle in the way of his dream. He allowed Scar to talk him out of what was rightfully his and a passion he wanted. Instead, he lowered his standards, became content and surrounded himself with individuals who neither had passions, standards, desires nor ambition. Truthfully, he surrounded himself with individuals who wanted nothing out of life. He allowed his current circumstance to become his vision.

In my years of working with individuals in the financial arena, one thing that is very apparent to me is that people know what they want in life but they just don't want it bad enough. This is evident when someone can tell you, with precise detail, about the home they want, the cars they desire and how it feels to drive them and even the amount of money they want to make. Yet, because they don't want it bad enough, they haven't taken the time to learn exactly what's required to obtain it and thereafter, do whatever else is required.

It's very simple. *Successful people do what unsuccessful people refuse to do.* You may tell me all day what you want in life but can I look at your actions and behavior to see that same picture? Never forget this,

"Behavior never lies." What you do tells the world exactly what you want in life. A man says he loves a woman but he mistreats her, a person says they want to improve their financial situation but does not learn about money or someone says they want to lose weight but refuses to exercise and change their eating. Their behavior tells you exactly what they really want out of life.

Chapter 2
The Shift

Later on in "The Lion King", The Pride Land became desolate. The village was running out of food because of the drought and poor leadership from Scar. Nala, the childhood friend Simba loved and played with when he was young, saw the village was dying and went hunting for food. While hunting she hears something in the bushes and attacks. After a brief fight, she is seen hovering over her adversary about to kill him and realizes it's Simba, the love of her life.

She was extremely disappointed he lost his will to win and left the village and his rightful place as king. After a long conversation with her, Simba still could not shake the mindset he was in and he resorted back to what he knew best, Hukuna Matata, which means no worries.

Over time, after having someone (Nala) with vision reminding him that it's never too late to become what you should have been, he began soul searching. The internal fight was strenuous and long. To clear his mind, he went to his secret place to rediscover who he was destined to become. During this time, his father, Mufasa, says these words to Simba that forever changes his life and destiny and those of others, "You are more than what you have become."

What he meant was this: There is greatness on the inside of you that everyone sees and understands *except* you. Therefore, you have not become what you were born to become. With his manhood, plus some challenges, Simba comes to himself and fights to resume the dream he allowed to die in his heart.

You must understand you are two people; the person you are currently and the person you are destined to become. The goal in life is to get those two people to meet. Never look at your past to determine your future. Your future is determined by what you decide to do today; it is like a clean white sheet of paper waiting to be written on by you.

You are like a dollar bill; your present condition does not determine your value. A dollar can be torn, dirty, ripped, missing a piece or two and smelly, but in its present condition what is it worth? It's still worth one dollar.

The lesson is simple: You are worth what you were when you were born – *Everything*. Like Simba, you need a friend that loves you enough to tell you the truth about your future in light of your present. You must believe your worst is over and your best is yet to come. Even after being told these things by those you love, you must believe it and act on it today. I believe in you, the question is do you believe in yourself? No matter how successful you become in life continue to tell yourself you can become more. Someone's destiny is tied to yours - if you lose they lose, if you win they win.

Chapter 3
Motivational Factors and Affirmations

Everyone has a motivating force within him or her. Money, family or friends motivate some, and some are motivated by positions. There are different motivations for every person. The reason why some motivational speakers work for some and don't work for others is motivation. You have to determine what motivates you. But without a goal, vision, and "date with your future", your motivation can fail.

People who lack motivation have not seen the potential of their future. Those who cannot see their future lack motivation. Most people you meet today are not excited about life. They don't enjoy life - they are simply enduring life. To be honest, most people actually hate their lives because they don't see things getting better. They have no drive, passion or motivation to make things happen in their lives, and all of their dreams and goals have been assassinated by life. They have grown comfortable in a situation they hate and it is reinforced or considered to be okay because everyone they know is in that same place of hopelessness.

Whenever I see people like this it tells me one important thing about them – they have not seen the potential of their future. Many are busy putting out the fires of their present and not taking the time to see the potential their future contains, thus settling for the pain of their present.

Do you talk to yourself on a daily basis? If so, is it positive or are you constantly telling yourself what you cannot do? If you fail to speak positive things into your own life daily, you will need to begin to do this to become mentally tough. Not only is this a requirement, you must also talk to yourself in the right way about the right things. The key is not what you say in the midst of the crowds but rather what you say to yourself when you are all alone with your situation. Remember, if you do not believe in yourself or do things to motivate yourself, how will you get others to do it?

In the midst of an excited and motivated crowd we all feel like a Super-Hero. Making powerful, positive confessions such as "I'm going to be a millionaire", "I will be debt free" or "I'm going to retire in 3 years" is easy to say in the moment. What if you could live in the moment all the time? What others say doesn't have nearly the long-term impact of what you say to yourself daily. What you ultimately do is determined by what you are saying to yourself when you are alone -- alone with your debts, alone with another rejection letter, or alone with your past. What will you say when you are alone?

Here are some of the things I say to myself daily regardless of how I feel or what's going on. Of course, it's easier to say these things when life is great but I say them to myself each day, allowing them to empower every part of my body. I say:

* I am a world changer.
* I can do all things.
* I can overcome all challenges.
* Every problem has a solution.
* I will be the person who will change someone's tomorrow.

You must understand your world is framed by you. Your present situation may appear void, without form and in darkness but there is a solution. The only way you can change your current situation is by first changing your words. It's not an act of magic; instead, it's an act of agreement.

When we speak life into our future and surround ourselves with individuals who pursue their dreams; those who speak positively into our lives, goals and dreams, we come into agreement with these things and eventually have what was predetermined for us. As you speak something, your mind takes a picture and sees what you said. An easy example to illustrate is to say aloud, "Red sports car." Did you see what came to mind? A picture of a red sports car automatically came to mind. Just as our current world was framed by a spoken word through faith, we frame our future by speaking something and having faith to believe it will happen in our lives.

As you continuously say your goals and dreams aloud with consistency and passion, your mind does not know it was only a thought. Instead, your mind believes it was a command and now assumes the responsibility of figuring out a way to make your dreams and goals a reality. When this happens, you become inspired and creative thoughts are birthed in your mind. Your thoughts become seeds planted in the soil of your mind, thus giving birth to new and creative ideas.

Chapter 4
Make A Choice

Thoughts assemble to form a detailed plan that shows you what you should do and the results you should receive. When you have the plan, write it down immediately. Now you have everything you need to walk into your destiny.

Simba made a choice to change after speaking to his father and realizing he was far greater than his present circumstances. He put a plan in place that wasn't perfect, but he believed in the plan and the outcome if he walked into his destiny. After returning from his time with his father, something in the atmosphere immediately changed. In fact, Rafiki, the wise baboon, went ahead of him to set the stage and guide Simba back to the path he was meant to follow. The major factors to the sudden change in Simba's situation was he said his goal and dream aloud, he connected with someone who believed in him and he took action.

Choose one thing in your present you want to change in your future and start changing what you say about it (what you say and what you do must be consistent). See yourself *doing* what you say and start *doing* it today.

You have hidden potential that's only released by your spoken words. Everything in life is created twice, but first it's created in your mind. The things you see now all started in someone's mind and they harvested those thoughts and ideas into a tangible form. The same is also true for your goals and dreams. Remember, everything that appears started as an unseen reality.

Don't Quit Too Soon

Before modern medicine, there was a woman who had a terrible disease that, in her day, meant an automatic death sentence. Her body was ill and she could have easily given up not knowing if she would meet the man that had the cure to her disease. She spent everything she had on doctors and professionals but her situation became worse. There was only one person in the entire world that knew how to cure her disease but she had not met him and had no idea where he was.

For 12 years, she lived with this dreaded disease that drained the life out of her daily, forcing her not to be touched by anyone. Imagine the turmoil this woman endured. If you truly think about it, most of us can't handle setbacks for one year before giving up on something, let alone twelve.

What kept her going? Daily she would say within herself, "I'm going to find the person who has the cure for my disease and I will live and not die. If I can just meet this man my life will change." These words and these words alone sustained her for 12 years. She believed, she kept moving, kept living and kept taking action. What will you say to yourself daily that will fuel you to never quit? What do your words do for you?

Part Two: Motivation And Mental Toughness

Chapter 5
Motivated To Win

Everyone should posses a plan that provides them the possibility to live their dream life. Many people discuss and talk about the things they want out of life but few do the single most important thing to achieve them and that is to create the plan. Do you have this plan? If not, you will become like the millions of people on this earth whose dreams die daily and within time forget you ever had any.

I know you have dreams but have you taken the time to outline, specifically, what you need to do to obtain those dreams and who is required in life to help you? In the next 3 days you must create your Dream Machine – the specific things you must do to live your dream life. *You must be willing to participant in your own rescue.*

Below you will find a great foundation to build upon when considering your Dream Machine plan. Create this dream plan now. Don't create it based on where you presently are financially. Instead, create it based on where you want to go financially.

* **Step One - Mindset:** The Trash must be removed and you must learn to think opposite of the masses.
* **Step Two - Create a Cash Flow System:** Learn to run your personal finances like a highly successful business.
* **Step Three - Create Money by Better Managing Money:** Create money with things you have like taxes, expenses or debt.
* **Step Four - Eliminate Debt:** Eliminate all debt to increase cash flow by 30-50%.
* **Step Five - Acquire assets "on sale":** Assets make you money with little or none of your involvement. Acquire them!
* **Step Six - Environment:** Create or join a group of like-minded individuals who are achieving the very goal you want to achieve.
* **Step Seven - Mental Toughness:** You must believe it's never too late to become what you should have been.

When you begin to embrace, touch or experience your future, it will provide you with all of the passion, drive and motivation you need to deal with the pain of your present. You must receive a daily dose of your future to push you past both the external and internal opposition. It is the potential of your future that keeps failure from being an option.

I'm not really sure who has the greatest imagination, my business partner or me. All I know is we both need our imagination to experience something neither of us has ever experienced before. *Imagination allows you to visit your future so you are motivated to leave your present.*

Taking Out The Trash

It's time to learn to play again. When you were a child, you didn't have money but you did have an imagination. With your imagination you became whatever you desired because you saw yourself differently from the way you really were. Your imagination allowed you to see yourself in your future regardless of your present. Become a child again and allow your imagination to motivate and show you the potential of what you can become.

Daily, sow into your future, so when you arrive at your future, it's not a repeat of your present. Are you so busy putting out fires in your present you fail to take time to work on creating a better future? This is the life of most people. They have allowed their lives to become so complex that they are busy but accomplishing nothing. Simplify your life so you can work on your future.

Busy people are broke people who live beneath their potential. Busyness can become so addictive that when you are not doing something, you feel guilty and unproductive thus you begin doing actions that lead you nowhere. To take control of your life you must first take control of your time. Daily, you must have a "date with your future." This is a standard time you are alone and you work on specific areas that will enhance your future. This is the birthing place for new ideas. Therefore no texting, no IM, no Social Networks and no phone calls. Instead, have a single focus on your future without distractions. Here are some things I work on.

First, I created a chart. It's a simple visual plan for me to constantly review and work from. Each day I have a "date with my future" so naturally I chart out the days of the week. Next, I put down what my subject or project is that I want to focus on. For instance, on Mondays, I will work on Internet Marketing. Under the Notes section I jot down what I need to focus on for that subject. I want to continuously make that aspect better and stay on top of it. So on Mondays, I focus on building a better list to market via the Internet. I also work on how to better leverage myself using Internet Marketing. The key to making this time productive is, for example, I don't allow distractions of Personal Development (Wednesday's focus) to get in the way when I am taking those 15 minutes or more to work on Internet Marketing.

Remember, I have a date with my future each day by visiting my chart and focusing on that day's subject. This way, I am sowing into my future daily.

Think about your future. Start out with seven major things you need to focus on each week for your future. Creating a chart will allow you to stay focused and motivated because you continuously refer to it each day and become motivated to reach your passion.

Day	Subject Of The Day	Notes (Focus Question)
Monday	Internet Marketing	How do I build a better list and create better leverage?
Tuesday	Creating Money	How do I use what I have to create what I need?
Wednesday	Personal Development	What is my passion and how will I perfect it?
Thursday	Cash Flow	Which expenses can I eliminate, reduce or make tax deductible?
Friday	Problem Solving	Create or review my plan to solve current or new problems.
Saturday	Financial Literacy	Review books, audios, seminars and notes to create new sources of money
Sunday	Review Ideas	Study my "idea bank" to see if any are ready to be converted into an asset.

If you commit 15 minutes to several hours of your life daily to work on your future, your life must change. Remember, this date occurs on holidays, vacation and even on your birthday. Through this "date with your future", you may finally decide to "Marry your purpose." A standard time you have allocated each day to work on perfecting your passion gives you a great advantage over conquering your fears. Success awaits those who will discover and perfect their passion so create your dates now.

New Glasses

Have you ever looked at something for the 100th time and then you see it? You see something different you've never seen before that has the ability to enhance your life? Actually, what you're seeing hasn't changed but you have changed. You are now thinking, understanding and perceiving at a higher level than you were a short time ago. This is a great sign your mind is growing and expanding because you are learning.

Children understand this when adults don't. A child will watch the same DVD one hundred times and look at it as if they are seeing it for the first time. However, each time they see it, they understand more and see something they missed the first time. But adults will read a book, review a business proposal or look at a principle and assume they have complete understanding the first time – IMPOSSIBLE!

It is critical that as you learn more, you review the same information over again until you obtain understanding so well that it's easy to create strategies that create freedom. This is why I strongly recommend spending time with your future. Each week you visit your future, your mind will begin to expand and cause you to see new and exciting possibilities you've never seen before.

Train your mind to think by setting aside time daily to do it and after a while it becomes natural. Create folders on your computer to collect ideas from various sources (seminars, books, thinking, internet, movies, and friends) then categorize them by major category and place into files. The key is going to be to set aside a standard time to review them and convert into an asset. Ideas create assets that create money. More importantly, solutions create freedom of the mind to create assets.

Family Motivation

I look at my family and say, "If I lose, they lose!" I love my family too much to fail them or even allow them to live a life that's beneath their potential. I will win because they desire to win. It's not the government or anyone else's job or responsibility to provide for my family; that's my divine assignment.

I focus on the result of winning and the impact it has on the next generation's life. I understand that my children's life will begin where mine ends. This is what I constantly tell myself: *If you are willing to spend two years of your life like others WON'T, you can spend the rest of your life like others CAN'T!!*

Two years can rewrite your entire family legacy. It could rewrite it so much that your great-great grandchildren may feel like they know you. Two years of intensified focus on learning, perfecting your passion and building a business could allow you to live like most people never even dream of living. Are you willing to sacrifice two years of your life for a lifetime of freedom?

Here is one of the most important questions you will ever be asked in your lifetime and the quality of your life and your children's life will be determined by your answer: "What do you want so bad in life you refuse to live without it and you are willing to sacrifice everything you have to achieve it?"

Everything in this world has a purpose in failure. Most people think the purpose of failure is to cause fear and keep them afraid of attempting something they want to do in life. Failure must be viewed differently if you are going to succeed or obtain your dreams. In fact, failure is a catalyst that helps you succeed. It shows you what will happen if you lose focus, quit, don't follow the plan or keep yourself motivated.

It's like in the movie "It's a Wonderful Life" with Jimmy Stewart. He was able to see how terrible things turned out for his family and others if he received his wish and was never born. He was discouraged because his business affairs were at the bottom and he wanted to quit. After seeing what would have happened or how bad things would have been without him, this insight provided him with the motivation required to deal with life's present struggles.

"I want it now!" is the cry of people who are full of potential, struggle their entire life to make ends meet and never become what they were born to become. You must decide what you would *like* to have versus what you would *love* to have. People never distinguish the two thus they exchange their life for things they *like* without understanding; if they had taken the time to learn the difference and pursued things they *loved*, these would have ultimately created the things they desired.

The lack of sacrifice consumes so much of your resources causing many to bury the dreams you *love*. The immediate gratification of the things you *like* such as an expensive new car, eating out at upscale restaurants or those designer outfits, further places the things you *love* on hold. Now, when you are a little older and come to yourself, you realize you have been pursuing a nightmare instead of a dream.

It may seem like the hole you've dug is so deep that pursuing things you love is almost impossible. However, it's never too late. Wake up and make the shift! Begin to defer the things you *like* in order to create things you *love*. Things such as living debt free, becoming an entrepreneur, buying real estate or pursuing your passion is possible for you. Things you *love* may not create money now but it creates a fortune later which allows you to obtain those things you *like* when you can most afford them and are mature enough to handle them.

If you pursue things you *like* first, they will rob you of the ability to obtain what you *love* later. They allow you to fill up your present while you empty your future. You can have them both; just obtain them in the right order. Remember these simple rules:

* Things I *like* fill up my present while robbing my future.
* Things I *love* empty my present while filling up my future.

You must decide which rule you will live by. What are you willing to give up to obtain your dream? Sacrifice is the ability to give up something you like, to create something you love.

Chapter 6
Surround Sound

I surround myself with passionate people whose dreams are bigger than mine. Being around passionate people with vision not only energizes me but it also helps me take the limits off of my life. When I am around this group, here are the principles that explode inside of me:

Principle #1 - Never tell me the sky is the limit when there are footprints on the moon. With the proper mindset and mentors, regardless of where your life is presently, your possibilities are limitless. You are one idea or one person away from resources that could change the legacy of your family and those of others. Will your great-great grandchildren remember your name because they saw your footprints?

Principle #2 - You are more than what you have become. You are two people: The person you are currently, and the person you are destined to become (as previously mentioned). The goal in life is to get those two people to meet. No matter how successful you become in life, continue to tell yourself you can become more. Someone's destiny is tied to yours. If you win, they win.

Principle #3 - You must see with your mind, what most people miss with their eyes. The worst vision in the world is 20/20. It only allows you to see what is seen. Everything in life is created twice, but first in your mind. Before you can ever begin to see with your mind you must remove the trash from years of being brainwashed. First, start by monitoring what you allow to enter your mind daily. Next, identify the limiting or fearful thoughts that come up in your mind. These limiting thoughts must be attacked and eliminated.

Principle #4 - Never shrink your dreams to fit your income. What you presently make has no impact on the dreams you can obtain. Many individuals reduce or shrink their dreams so that it comfortably fits or can be obtained within their salary. No! Allow your dreams and the pursuit of them to determine the size of your income. If your dreams don't require the help of others, your dream simply isn't big enough. The first step in changing your income is changing your words and actions.

* Your income should never determine your dream. Allow your dream to determine your income.

* Determine what a dream life looks like to you. If you think on it long and hard enough, your brain will find away to achieve it.

* Expand your dream daily by visiting your future, being around people with bigger dreams and by changing your environment.

Principle #5 - Those who have something you don't have, know something you don't know. You want more in life, don't you? Have you seen people who have what you want? Well, they simply know things you presently don't know and therefore do things you presently don't do. They may know how to connect with the right people, negotiate the deal, and inspire people to follow them or build a business. All of these things at one time they didn't know, but they learned each of them. If it's been done before that means you can do it too.

Principle #6 - Look at your friends and decide if they are assets or liabilities. I'm going to ask you to do one of the most difficult things you have ever done in your life. It will require you to be honest with yourself because what you're about to do will determine the quality of your future and that of your children.

Look at each one of your friends (people who you spend time with and impact your life) and determine if they are an asset or a liability? People are assets if they are helping you or can help you fulfill your dreams. They're a liability if they are not and cannot help you fulfill your dreams.

Some of your best friends are liabilities. They drain you of your money, your motivation and your inspiration to be great. You love being around them because they are funny, they know how to have a good time and you just enjoy their company, but they cannot contribute to your greatness. If you want them in your life but you also want your goals and dreams, here is my recommendation: *If you cannot influence your friends, it's time to change your friends!* If they are unwilling to remove the trash in their mind and think at a higher level, they can no longer be your best friend.

Ok, it's time to evaluate your friends. Again, this is one of the toughest things you will do in life so don't rush through it nor procrastinate to do it. It will become a defining moment in your life.

The Friend	Asset	Liability	Why?

At times your best friend is your worst enemy. Look at the last 5 calls to your cell phone or your 5 closest friends. The average of their lives or income is what you are becoming. Is that what you want? Again, look at your friends and decide are my friends assets or liabilities. Assets are people who challenge you to obtain your dream and liabilities are people who "lie about your ability" and say with words or actions you'll never do it! Has your best friend become your worst enemy?

Principle #7 - The only limitation you have in life is the way you think. Let's say you have past failures, you lack a graduate degree or your life right now is in chaos. None of these situations limit what you can achieve in life. Your success in life is determined primarily by one thing and that's how you think. No other one single factor has more influence as to what you will achieve in life. Daily you must work on thinking at a higher level (get that trash out). One of the ways I practice thinking at a higher level is by starting each day with mental training from the world's greatest Book.

Success comes with a very expensive price tag – money, time, disappointment, and then there is failure. But embrace hope and understand that some things you must learn to succeed can't be taught to you by anyone or found in a book. They must be obtained in the pain of your failure. *Failure creates focus and focus creates fortunes.*

Here are some things I learned in my failures.

* God does not trust what time has not tested. Never allow a person to enter your inner circle until they have been with you a while so you can observe their loyalty in various situations. Trust must be earned.

* Never take advice from those who are not in the game. If a person wants to give you advice on how to pursue your passions, make money or build a business but they're not pursuing their dreams, what can they tell you? A person who isn't in the game is disqualified from giving you advice.

* People must be willing to participant in their own rescue. If you want a person to succeed more than they do for themselves, you are going to spend a lot of time trying to help a person who does not really want help.

* Never start a business without having the assistance of someone who has successfully done what you want to do. The money you pay them for their wisdom, insight and contacts are to be viewed as an investment never an expense.

* Business is a team sport. To be successful in business you must have a team of competent people who you trust, people who know what you don't know and people who are as driven to succeed as you are. What do you want to be bigger in life, your ego or your paycheck? Remember, one is too small of a number for greatness. Even the greatest man that walked on earth had a team of 12.

Whenever a successful person experiences failure, the first thing they look for is not someone to blame but instead, the lessons to be learned so they can succeed.

Principle #8 - People who see nothing, do nothing and therefore have nothing! If you believed no matter how hard you worked or what you did your life wouldn't change, what would you do? Nothing! So, when you see people who are doing nothing you already know what they believe. But what if you believed, by better managing your time, building a business, learning to better manage your money or pursuing your passion, life has a limitless amount of opportunities? What would you do? What you believe impacts what you do which determines what you have.

Principle #9 - If you see what others don't see you can have what others don't have. When a problem arises such as the stock market going down or unemployment on the rise, most of the individuals around you see the same thing – misery! However, you see opportunities because this is what you are trained to look for.

For example, if a job lay-off occurs, between unemployment, proper utilization of retirement, severance pay and becoming a part-time consultant for the former employer, this could provide someone 12 months of not having to work for money. You view this as an opportunity to work on building your dreams and getting paid to do it.

By seeing something different, you now have what others never will until they change what they see.

Principle #10 - You can't make right decisions with wrong information. Decision-making is only effective when you have the proper information that allows you to make an informed decision. Think about it. If I asked you if I could visit on tomorrow and you said yes, but I never told you I would be knocking at your door at 5 a.m., you may not have said yes. While the example is trivial, I think you get my point. Before making any decision, make sure you have all of the necessary information to make an informed decision.

The Underdog

I enjoy attending movies with great music where the underdog wins. While I'm viewing the movie, I see myself as the central character. I embrace the events as if they are happening in my life – the pain, the betrayal, the fear but most of all the victory. I will relive the movie again and again until it becomes a part of me. The movie becomes real to my situation. While others are there for the enjoyment, I am there for something totally different. I am there for the inspiration and the lesson that life again wants to teach me - **Never quit you were born to win!**

How you think when you lose determines how long it will be before you win. No matter how great a person each of us is, we are going to lose (disappointment) at some point in time. The key is how this will impact your thinking. Will you begin to say, "I knew I couldn't do it so why did I even try?" or will you say to yourself, "Because I'm a winner and I'm supposed to win, it can't be over so let's do it again."

A tough-minded individual is a person who, during adversity, is able to increase their focus, drive, determination and will to win. When things are at their worst you must be at your best. Even while you are losing you are already thinking about how you will win the next one and the lessons you will learn from this loss to win. You haven't ignored the fact you lost, but you found the "good" in the "bad" that will make you "great." Your thoughts are, "I lost" not that "I am a loser", "I Failed", not that "I am a failure", or "This is just a temporary situation subject to change without notice" not "This just must be my life story."

We have been programmed to fail by seeing things from a negative perception by this impoverishing system. We are trained to always focus or find the things we don't have thus becoming discouraged. Ask most people who are living payday to payday a simple question, "Do you want your financial situation to change?" Here is the exact response you will get: "Yes, but I don't make enough, my credit is bad, I have too much debt, I don't have any money in the bank, my spouse won't work with me, all my family members struggle too and the economy is bad."

None of these excuses have anything to do with the question. Notice the first response is always about what I don't have. After listing all of these things, do you understand why people are now discouraged and have talked themselves out of their situation changing? *You will never move beyond your excuses.*

The correct response should have been, "Yes, I want my situation to change and I'm taking inventory of what I have or have access to in order to make the change." Here are some things most people have that could be used to solve the problem of living payday to payday.

* **Passion or talent** - Convert it into a business.

* **Internet access** - Market the newly created business on the Internet to millions of people for less than $100 per month.

* **Debt** - Reduction or elimination of debt creates money.

* **Taxes** - Get your refund in your check now in addition to doing some tax planning.

* **Credit** - Enhance your scores to create money (generally speaking, a 1% decline in interest rate on a $200k loan reduces your payment $200 per month) and create access to the bank's money to help you fund your dreams.

* **Relationships** - Find people who know what you don't know. Help them make money now and they will help you build an asset you never could have built alone.

* **Expenses** - Without cutting life, reduce expenses. What if you reduced 10 items $10 per month? That's $100 monthly tax-free.

* **Time** - Use your time to learn what you presently don't know.

Of the 8 things mentioned, it's easy to say which ones you can't do. Instead, find the 3 or 4 you can do and allow them to create what you don't have.

Keep Fear Away

Fear causes people to live in a place they hate. It keeps them from doing things they know they really need to do to improve their lives. Everyone knows the story of David and Goliath. Here are some keys points you may not remember which brings to light this principle so well. The trained army, who was supposed to fight Goliath, after seeing him, was afraid and ran from him.
And, David overcame his fear to fight Goliath after he heard about the reward. The reward was so motivating that he asked to hear about it again. Maybe he needed to hear it again to overcome his fear or maybe he needed to hear it again as motivation. Regardless, the reward was if he defeated Goliath he would receive 1) the king's daughter, 2) his family would pay no taxes, and 3) the king will make him rich.

There was a risk involved but it was the reward that motivated David to take action. I want you to consider this before launching out into a new opportunity. Ask yourself, "If the cost to seize the opportunity is $1,000 what's the most I can lose? Now what's the most I can make?" It's unlimited!

The risk is limited to $1,000 but the potential reward is unlimited. I always think about this to help me overcome fears and seize new opportunities. Remember, whenever you are about to move into a new venture ask yourself these two questions:

* What's the most I can lose and if I lose, can I deal with it?
* What's the most I can gain and if I made that amount, would my life change significantly and help me change the lives of others?

If the amount you can lose is limited and the amount you can gain is unlimited, why are you afraid to take the limited risk?

Fear does have positive attributes as well. Fear is good when it keeps you focused. Imagine in 30 days, 12 months or in 5 years you are the same person you are today. No growth, no improvement and no closer to your dreams. *Allow this fear of staying the same to motivate you to greatness.* If you allow this type of fear to control your actions as you have allowed other fears to do, this will serve as a catalyst to motivate you to passionately pursue your dreams and become great.

Each time you want to quit, close your eyes and see yourself 10 years older in the exact same situation you are presently. Feel the frustration, disappointment and emptiness. It's a different feeling to be broke or not know your purpose and passion at 20 but at 40 the feeling is called DEPRESSION! If you can consistently embrace that feeling today it will create a fear that will not allow you to fail. The only fear that should control your life is the fear of not changing daily; changes that move you one step closer to who you were born to become. Remember this principle: *If the potential reward is great, don't be afraid to take the limited risk.*

Fundamental Reading

I read a lot of books about failure creating success. Books allow you to learn from the author and use their sacrifice, knowledge and wisdom to educate you about different topics. The great part of this is while it may have taken them years to understand the lessons taught you could learn those same lessons in a matter of days. Their failure was a key ingredient in their success. Use their story to see your situation as only an ingredient instead of a recipe.

Many times, when you attend a powerful seminar, read a great book or listen to an awesome CD, you now want to change the world. But how long do you feel that way? You started making changes as you learned but things are not changing as quickly as you hoped or more obstacles than you expected seem to arise and you are not sure what to do to keep from becoming discouraged. So now, what do you do?

Learn to finish what you start but only start those things that are worth finishing. Why spend so much of your life starting things you will never finish and wasting valuable time that should have been spent on something you were passionate about? How do you separate yourself from the masses that start things but never finish them?

* Make sure it is consistent with or fuels your passion.
* Schedule time daily to work on it.
* Create a plan that ensures success.
* Have a team that keeps your creative juices flowing.
* Become accountable to a mentor or a friend who cares more about your future than your feelings.

As a good parent you require or required your children to finish what they started (e.g. those violin lessons) because you said it builds character and makes them a better person. Doesn't this advice hold true even as an adult?

Chapter 7
Mental Toughness

Have you ever seen or known someone who just refused to lose? All indications around them such as the sells report, cash flow, or the clients that left them, clearly showed they were losing but somehow, in their mind, they still saw themselves as not only a winner but as winning. It's like they don't have another option or a Plan B. Even at their darkest hour when even the most loyal people walk out on them, the thought of quitting, stopping and not pressing on seemed as if it never crossed their mind.

Mentally tough individuals never live in a make-believe world that denies the facts or what is seen, instead they seem to always be moved or controlled by that which is unseen. What do these people possess that others don't seem to have? How did they obtain this "whatever" that drives them? How do they keep themselves motivated, encouraged, focused or driven even in the worse of situations or times; situations they clearly don't understand?

When others are looking for an exit, these individuals are looking for solutions because they believe every problem has a solution. When tough situations arise and it seems by all accounts they should be running away, these individuals run toward the obstacle with everything they have. In the midst of adversity, these individuals do what others can't seem to do or choose not to do. What do they know or see that only a select few individuals seem to know and understand?

What Is Mental Toughness

Mental toughness is the ability to increase your intensity, focus, and drive to obtain your goal in the midst of adversity. When things are at their worst, you are at your best. Let's look at 8 principle mindsets of mentally tough people.

Principle Mindset #1 - They live as if the boats have been burned and fighting is the only viable option. The story is told of Napoleon leading his men into battle against the enemy who were on an island. Napoleon was losing the battle but he still loaded his men onto boats to pursue them to the island. Upon arriving on the island he burned the boats to the dismay of his troops. He then stated to them, "We have but one option and that is to fight and win." The tough-minded person views adversity the same way.

Principle Mindset #2 - They believe they were born to do what they are doing and they have been predestined to win. Over one million sperm race towards the egg to become fertilized to create a living being. The fact you were born proves you are a winner because you beat millions of others. Tough-minded people understand there was a reason they were born and regardless of what happens in life, they will become successful. They were born for this reason and they have been fully equipped to finish what they started.

Principle Mindset #3 - The Vantage Point. They see themselves winning when others see them losing. At times, to a fault, a tough-minded person can actually be losing and everyone one around them sees it from their vantage point. Just like in the movie *Vantage Point*, everyone saw the same event (the President being assassinated), however they all witnessed it from a different perspective thus their stories were vastly different. The tough-minded person will never deny the facts of the situation they are facing but they will see it from a different vantage point, and see something entirely different from what others see. An outsider will say, "You are losing; you must quit." However, the tough-minded says, "I'm losing but I have found a way to win." The tough-minded person never denies the facts but because of where they stand, they see things differently.

Here is a simple example. Imagine you are in a seminar and at the front of the room is the presenter (tough-minded person). You both are in the same room and see some of the same things, mainly items to the left or right of each of you. However, there are things the teacher sees that you don't see such as the doors you entered through or the persons sitting behind you. Tough-minded people see things from a different vantage point.

Principle Mindset #4 - Live with a Solution Mentality. When something adverse happens, many are quick to identify or point out all of the problems. Most people are really good at it. Why? They have been trained to see the problems and then complain about them. The tough-minded people always look for solutions after understanding there is a problem. This is how they have trained their minds from years of solving problems.

Principle Mindset #5 - Believe if I don't complete the task, someone whom I love will suffer. Relationships and family are extremely important to the tough-minded person and they understand if they quit or lose, someone important to them will also lose. Therefore, losing is no longer, and has never been, an option to them. To obtain additional motivation they are able to feel the pain, frustration and disappointment of the people they love and it creates an additional catalyst for them to win.

Principle Mindset #6 - They understand some things they need to learn in life to succeed can only be learned in their temporary failure. Tough-minded people fail a lot in life but they are not failures because of how their failures make them successful. They understand the key lessons that are a requirement for success cannot be learned any other way but through failure. Mentors can't teach it, seminars can't prepare you nor can you experience it by reading every book.

Failure is necessary for success. Failure makes you more focused, it breaks you like a bone to become stronger, it removes the embarrassment of making mistakes, it allows you to taste defeat and to hate the very smell, or it humbles you. It's possible that all of the above could happen but tough-minded people understand it's required.

It's not just the failure that's required, but it's the lessons you are willing to learn when you fail. It's hard to face a crushed dream because it's so painful but you find a number of lessons from it. You know you must, like a crime scene, examine everything closely to find the evidence that helps you to solve this crime against your potential. *You must face it before you can fix it!*

Principle Mindset #7 - Stubborn. Tough-minded people are stubborn when necessary but are always open to new ideas. After working through their plan and it is not working, they will stop, reassess and find a better way. Thomas Edison attempted to invent the light bulb and after thousands of failures simply said, "I also discovered thousands of ways not to do it." He was a tough-minded person and realized in his failures, his current process wasn't the way to do it so he began finding the right way because he was destined to do it.

Principle Mindset #8 - They are finishers in a world of starters. Before a tough-minded person starts anything, one of their questions to themselves is "Am I willing to finish what I start?" Unlike 98% of the population, they are finishers. They understand that if they allow or accept not finishing into their lives, it will shape their destiny. They remember *a man does not decide his future, instead he decides his habits and his habits decide his future.*

Chapter 8
One Of The Best Examples

I looked at Napoleon, Winston Churchill, great athletes and world-changing businessmen, but it wasn't until I was in church one Sunday and the minister began to talk about a guy named Paul, the Apostle Paul, who truly defined the meaning of mental toughness and motivation for me. I'm not a Bible scholar, but there were some things that were said about him as he embraced a cause (dreams and goals) he was willing to die for.

Paul was a man with a mission, and although he didn't realize he was the person for it at first, others saw it in him. Once he realized it for himself, his mental toughness had to kick in. He began to embrace and focus on it. Paul considered his cause worth sacrificing everything for. And he pushed and pressed his way through some difficult times until he reached his goal.

Once Paul began working towards his passion or cause, of course hardships came. It is impossible to obtain goals without some obstacles at some point. A good soldier always endures hardships. Paul, however, didn't allow outside distractions to come between where he was and where he was going. Paul's passion and mission brought him near death experiences, wrongful prison sentences, and people not believing in him. He endured being homeless and many sleepless nights all while being in the midst of his dreams and goals. Does any of that sound familiar?

Through it all, his concern remained on his dreams. Yes, there were times when he changed his plans but he changed them, not stopped them. His mental toughness would not allow him to stop and that decision ultimately led him to success.

Paul didn't reach his mission by influence alone, thinking alone, or sticky notes alone. He reached it by making a decision that no matter what hardships came his way, he would stay committed to his passion. He shared what he learned with everyone he came in contact with to help others who may have been experiencing what he had already endured. He shared the trials, the abuse and the joys of seeing his hard work come to pass so that it could encourage others. He believed in his destiny and was determined to complete it. He was consistent, courageous and committed.

As you can imagine, I was blown away by all the lessons I was taught. The most important lesson was very simple – Life without a purpose is a tragedy! Here are five more lessons to embrace and consider.

Lesson One - Mentally tough people embrace their goals and dreams by pouring their life into it. You must be willing to spend all of your resources to fulfill your dreams and if there ever comes a point that required you to walk in the opposite way of those closest to you, at least you did it to embrace your life's purpose. You see it's not about you. Instead, it's about your willingness to change the legacy of those around you. The greatness of a man is not what he does but rather what he does for others. Find your purpose and sacrifice everything for it. Until you find your purpose, you will always leave room to quit!

Lesson Two - Keep the reward in front of you. Mentally tough people are controlled by the outcome. You have to clearly see, embrace and become fully persuaded of the reward you'll receive once your dreams and goals are fulfilled. It's important that you visit your future so much that your reward becomes real; so real that you talk as if you already possess the reward.

Lesson Three - You were born to fulfill the assignment and purpose God has given you. It's important to believe you received this God-given right to do what you do with the full backing, support and endorsement of Almighty God.

Lesson Four - He believed in divine assistance. Anything that opposes your assignment and purpose opposes God.

Lesson Five - You must believe you will win regardless of how bad things may seem. Even when you're struggling, it's a necessary process for you to win. Even when you're down, you have to view it as if you're watching that same movie for the 100th time and you already know the outcome – YOU WIN! The bottom line is simple. Life without a purpose is a tragedy!

How does this relate to us? How do you to become mentally tough?

In defeat, set back or failure, take the time to address the obstacles that occurred in your life. Analyze, learn and study the situation to better prepare yourself for future adversity. Unlike others, don't avoid the pain of the situation. Instead, embrace the pain until it hurts so bad that you know you never want to feel the pain again. Carry this feeling with you through life as a reminder of what happens to people who refuse to win. This pain does not make you bitter; it makes you better. It's a constant reminder of why you must stay focused and what life can quickly become when you are not focused.

Find things you love and practice giving them up. Build from small items to bigger items. Imagine you are in a difficult situation (e.g. lost job, home in foreclosure or business deal loses a lot of money). Create the environment and mindset that these events are happening in your life and aggressively move into the plan of action that is necessary to win. Feel the pain of the situation to increase your intensity as you take action. Put pressure on yourself so that when opposition actually comes, you are more than ready. Being tough-minded is a process – a required process to succeed. Without becoming tough-minded you will quit on the dreams you love and were born to fulfill.

Daily Affirmation: If I am willing to spend two years of my life like others won't, I can spend the rest of my life like others can't."

Never tell me the sky is the limit when there are footprints on the moon. The sky is not the limit, if so we never would have gone to the moon. With the proper mindset and mentors, regardless of where you are presently in life, your possibilities are limitless. You are one idea or one person away from resources that could change the legacy of your family and those of others. Will your great-great grandchildren remember your name because they see your footprints (i.e. businesses you left them, stocks you purchased or real estate)?

The major problem that must be addressed is the *trash*, that's right, the *trash* in your mind. It is this *trash* that keeps the majority of people living in a place they hate, struggling financially and unhappy most of their lives. This *trash* has been placed inside of you by your parents, your teachers, your friends, the media and finally by you. You have been around *trash collectors* the majority of your life and now have convinced yourself, where you are in life is where you are suppose to be, so you accept it.

This is what the *trash* sounds like that most people accept as the normal way of thinking:

* My job is my major and only source of income. I will have debt all of my life.

* I've made too many mistakes in my past to fulfill my purpose.

* Starting a business is too risky. I'll just keep my secure job (your friend just got laid off after working 20 years and you still believe this way).

* I don't have a college degree.

* I need two incomes to make it.

* You need money to make money. Besides, I don't have what it takes to succeed.

* I need extra money so I need to get a part-time job.

If you are thinking, "All of what you just said sounds right" that means the *trash* has impacted what you believe is possible in your life. You must embrace people who are taking action; people who are saying and believing, "All things are possible to them that believe" - **I believe!** What a person believes is real becomes their reality.

Part Three: Financial Principles

Chapter 9
Financial Principles

The number one reason people struggle financially is because they do not invest in their financial literacy. People spend at least eight hours a day working for money, but they spend no time daily learning how money works. Ask most people which of the following they have spent the least amount of money on in the past 90 days – food, clothing, personal care, or financial literacy. The answer will always be financial literacy. Why? Our schools don't teach it. They teach us how to work for money but they never teach us how money works.

When you work for money, you (the employee) are fulfilling the dreams of others while your dreams die daily. Eventually you forget you ever had a dream. When you improve your financial literacy, you stop making mistakes that take a lifetime to correct. Without financial literacy people never learn the difference between assets and liabilities. They spend their entire lives accumulating liabilities, believing them to be assets.

Mark Twain said it best. "A formal education will make you a living while an informal education will make you a fortune." By reading books, listening to audios, attending seminars and having mentors, you will learn in a short period of time (with minimal cost), what it took others years or even a lifetime to learn. *The key to earning is learning!* Remember, the more you know about money, the easier it is to make money without having any money.

You must embrace the following statement in order to have personal and business success financially. The lack of understanding this statement will keep people in financial bondage more than anything else. *"When people struggle financially it is not because of money, it's because of what they don't know about money."* Let's look at several principals to help you become what you are destined to be.

Principle 1 – Money can't buy happiness, neither can poverty.In fact, poverty can't buy anything.

Have you ever come across a person who was wise but at the same time poor-minded? Their wisdom is powerful and moving yet no one remembers them or takes them seriously because they are poor-minded. Wisdom is better than strength; nevertheless the poor person's wisdom is ineffective because their words are not heard.

Though money can't buy happiness, it can buy food, clothing and other necessities of life. Having these things can make people happy and release them from depression. Only when depression is defeated can a person truly receive happiness and joy. Many people we desire to help have both financial and inner needs that must be met. After you have provided for their financial needs now you can effectively show and direct them to the true source of happiness – joy and inner peace.

Let's get real. There are happy people in this world, but their happiness is tied to temporal things that are subject to change without notice. Most people are happy when their bills are paid, there is money in the bank and they possess more than enough to provide for their family. When all of your needs are met, there is no need to choose between money and inner peace.

When you are poor, regardless of the amount of wisdom you have, it's hard to change the destiny of your family and have a major impact on the world. Poverty wages an enormous mental battle that distracts you from focusing on the truly important things in life. When you don't have money, every area of your life is affected adversely and you don't function at your best in any area of your life. When you lack money, you lack a powerful weapon that can be used against your legacy.

You must understand it is impossible to leave your job, anything rented or your experiences as an inheritance to your children. The mentality that says, "I can't take it with me anyway" and "Money isn't that important" has a detrimental impact on the legacy you leave for your family.

Poverty constricts channels of success and suffocates your destiny. Prosperity is more than money. It is allowing every area of your life to operate at its fullest potential and money certainly helps. Without money, your effectiveness of promoting your cause is limited. Always remember, the second greatest book that can impact a person's life is your checkbook.

Principle 2 – Money is only an idea and those who lack money simply lack ideas.

If you don't have money it's because you have been working more than you have been thinking. *Thinking is more difficult than working and that's why so few people do it.* Many have been conditioned to think that when they need money they should obtain a job. When we need money, we say we need to go and think.

Here are things people say that let me know they don't understand the value or power of thinking. "I'm too busy to think", "Thinking can't make me money" or "Thinking is for lazy people." If this is how you believe then we have some work to do. Here are some things to consider.

Stop seeking after money. What you need is a **S.I.P.** (no drinking permitted). **S**trategies - innovative ways to put ideas into an action plan. **I**deas - innovative ways to do things. **P**eople - individuals who know what you don't know.

Keep your life simple to avoid unnecessary clutter in your mind. Ideas cannot be birthed in a cluttered mind. Everything you now see was once someone's idea. Ideas energize, activate creativity and attract other ideas. Daily, have a standard time to think to harvest ideas and place them into an "Idea Bank." This is a folder on your computer where you keep all ideas to review and convert into assets in the near future.

A great example of one thing you must learn to do as you optimize your thinking time is to learn to analyze an opportunity. To be successful in life you must be open to new ideas and you must spend part of your day looking for them. There are numerous legitimate opportunities out there you will never see if you possess a "this is a scam" mentality or allow fear to control you. One of the best ways to begin creating the life you desire is to tap into your purpose and create a system to profit from it.

Principle 3 - A formal education will make you a living but an informal education will make you a fortune.

I believe if you give a person a light (education) they will find their way. I say this to stress that I believe strongly in education but it has to be the right type of education. You must have the right combination between a formal education (what you get from schools) and an informal education (what you learn from people who are successful doing what you have learned in your formal education).

What's the purpose of a formal education versus an informal education and does it really work?

The purpose of school (formal education) is to educate you to obtain a job and maintain a good standard of living. If 90% of people are struggling or living payday to payday, what does that say about our educational system? At the age of 65, after working 40 plus years, if these same 90% of people still need outside assistance to survive, what does this say about our formal education system? It says, to be successful, the formal education system must be combined with the informal education system.

Parents encourage their children to read a book a day but when was the last time the parent read a book? The point is, education doesn't end when you graduate from school (which most parents believe), but it now transitions from a formal education to an informal education.

It's what you learn after school that will determine your level of financial success. Parents must learn how to take what their children are learning in school and teach them how it applies to life. This is one of the key differences in the rich and the middle class. Their children (the rich), throughout their lives are receiving two educations at once. If you lack the ability to provide your children with this informal education you have three options:

* Don't provide it to your children and watch how they underachieve in life.

* Quickly get an informal education so you can teach them.

* You, along with your children, seek a mentor who can provide an informal education.

In summary, the formal education teaches you how to get a job, while an informal education teaches you how to manage the money from that job so you don't have to work the job until retirement because you have found better ways to create money. To be successful, the two must be combined into one.

Principle 4 - The system that impoverishes you can never empower you.

You are in warfare and the battleground is your mind. There are two systems. One is extremely aggressive, constantly bombarding you with its ideas and processes – it's the impoverishing system.

This system is designed to keep you with the masses of people who spend their entire lives struggling over money. It is estimated that 95%

of the world's population spend their entire lives controlled by the system. This impoverishing system brainwashes you to believe:

* Your job is your major and only source of income.
* You need to live on two incomes.
* Debt is a part of life.
* A business is too risky.
* Salary is to pay bills.
* Retire at age 65.
* Save if money is left over.
* Invest to earn 2-4% per year.

However, the lesser known of these two systems is the empowering system that does not pursue, but rather must be pursued. It's a system that when embraced, causes you to be ridiculed by the masses because they don't understand it and that's why they attack it. Here are some of the beliefs of this system. It's estimated that less than 5% of the world's population understands and follows this system:

* Multiple streams of income. Your job begins the streams and should position you to start additional streams.
* Debt freedom.
* A business is the best way to build wealth.
* Your salary should be used to buy assets "on sale."
* Retire young to retire rich.
* Savings is a bill.
* Invest to earn 5-7% per month.

The system you decide to live by will determine the quality of your life.

Principle 5 - Spending should be based on
your monthly savings, not your monthly income.

Lending institutions determine the amount of your loan and what they believe you can afford by your gross income and financial obligations (bills and debts). However, your personal ability to buy should be based on what you are consistently able to save for four to six months without the money, as if you were actually making a payment. This allows you to feel what it's like to have the monthly payment and related costs to determine if you can actually afford it. It also allows more time to set aside money for the down payment, which will mean a lower monthly payment and/or provides an emergency fund.

You should never expect others to do more for you than you are willing to do for yourself. It is important to know your purpose and the best way to fulfill your purpose. People who aren't sure about their purpose are prone to waste their life and their resources. Any person that can waste their life will also waste their life's earnings. By knowing your purpose, you can make purchases that are consistent with your purpose and propel you to your destiny. Think of it this way. If I hire you to wash my car, I will be more inclined to purchase supplies that will assist you in washing the car rather than supplies that would assist you in mowing the lawn.

Once you tap into your purpose, your income will certainly expand but the key is to base your spending on the amount of increased savings. An increase in income should always expand your vision, not your spending.

Principle 6 - If you are too busy to start a business, that means you are too busy making someone else rich.

During many of my speaking engagements, here is one of my favorite questions to ask (Fill in the blanks). People will say, "I don't have enough _____ and _____." There are millions of words that could have been selected but I always get the same answer "Time and Money." Why is that? People have become convinced "staying busy" means you're productive at your job or business and you're important.

Busy people always live beneath their potential. Inside most people are dreams and one of those dreams is to start your own business but many are too busy to do it because of their job or life. If you are too busy to start your own business or to learn to start your own business, you are spending the best years of your life making someone else rich, in every aspect of his or her life. What about yours?

Stop the madness and establish a standard time daily to work on your dream. You spend at least 8 hours a day working on another's dream, so can you give your dream at least one hour per day?

Someone will get wealthy off of your labor, so why shouldn't it be you? If you spent half the amount of time working on your future as you spend working on your employer's future, you can become successful. Schedule time daily to work on your dreams and business. Your passion is the perfect birthing place for your business.

Principle 7 - Savings is the one bill
most people are delinquent in paying.

If you asked the average person who's been working 5 years or more, if they have saved at least $1,000 for every year they have worked, most will tell you "No." That's less than $85 per month or about $21 per week! This happens because many people see savings as an event that should occur if there is money left over, when in fact it should be viewed as a bill to yourself that must be paid monthly, or better yet, each time you are paid.

You must "pay into your savings" with the same conviction you pay your bills. "Pay into your savings" by creating an automatic draft amount along with your bills so within time, you'll see it as one bill. Here is a basic principle you should follow: *Save it before you see it.* You should also consider the following:

* Save ½ of all raises.
* Create motivational reasons why saving is a requirement.
* Maximize your retirement accounts after you obtain understanding.
* If you withdraw money, consider it as loan you must pay back to yourself.

Once you obtain a conviction for saving, it becomes easier to take care of emergencies when they arrive without incurring debt. This will also allow you to take advantage of profitable opportunities and begin to invest.

Principle 8 - Never permit new
dreams to die because of old habits.

What do you want so badly in life you refuse to live without it? This becomes your dream and you should do whatever is necessary to obtain it. Your greatest enemy to you obtaining your new dreams will be old habits.

Old habits are things such as making excuses, mismanagement of time and money, not reading daily, associations with people who have no vision, not having "A date with your future", being too busy or quitting when opposition arises. These are just a few of the old habits that will keep you trapped in the pain of your present. Someone coined a powerful principle that applies here, *"A man doesn't decide their future, they decide their habits, and their habits decide their future."*

New dreams require new habits, and without new habits new dreams die and are discarded as past dreams have been. Don't allow this to happen. Feed your dreams to become stronger than reality. Dreams are fed by associating with others that have dreams and speak with passion about their dreams. Their passion ignites a greater passion in you concerning your dreams.

Pictures also feed a dream. They allow you to see what awaits you as you change those old habits. Finally, verbalization feeds your dreams. As you speak with passion, you now see and embrace the unseen each day. There is nothing like a dream to create a future. Keep this in mind. You know life is good when your reality is better than your dream. This is your outcome if you embrace NEW HABITS!

*Principle 9 - Only borrow when the return
is greater than that which you borrowed.*

When you borrow money, it must make you money. If it doesn't make you money, that means it's taking your money. If you had a friend who was taking your money, how long would they be your friend? You would call them a thief! Debt is a thief when it does not make you money. Don't borrow to impress others or to create a tax deduction. Borrow to buy assets on sale.

My definition of an asset is something that makes you money with little or none of your involvement. Just because it sounds like it may be an asset does not necessarily make it an asset. Here is what I mean:

* **Stocks:** They are an asset if they are making money right now. Learn the strategy called, Writing Covered Calls, where you rent your stocks out monthly to produce cash flow even if the stock price did not increase.

* **Rental Property:** This sounds like an asset, but is it making you money? After you pay the mortgage and other expenses, does it produce cash flow? Assume your mortgage plus other expenses are $500 and the rent is $800. This produces cash flow is $300. You borrow to gain positive cash flow. A home that has equity when you purchased it plus the tenant paying the debt for you is an ASSET!

* **Business:** Are you the business or does the business have systems to make money? Just having a business does make it an asset; it has to make money without you. To borrow $100,000 with a $1,000 per month payment for a business that pays you $5,000 per month is borrowing for a greater return.

Principle 10 - Understand it before you under take it.

If you don't understand something well enough to explain it someone else so they understand it, you don't understand it enough to invest your money. Without obtaining an understanding, how can you properly evaluate and analyze the opportunity? One mistake made as a result of not asking the right questions because you lack an understanding could create a situation that takes a lifetime to correct. Before you purchase something you don't really understand *your first step should be a second opinion!*

It doesn't matter if the sales person understands it, the lender understands it, or the financial advisor understands it, the key question is, do you understand it? Before obligating yourself, sit down with your spouse or a friend and explain it to them. If you can't get them to understand it that means you don't understand it, so don't move forward yet. Understand it before you do it to avoid a lot of frustration in your life.

Principle 11 - Without an emergency plan, everything becomes an emergency.

If you lost your job, how do you pay your bills? What is your written plan to handle unexpected expenses without paying bills late or incurring debt? Even though people understand and recognize these events are real possibilities, they never take the time to create a written plan to address them.

An old Proverb says *"A wise man foresees the difficulties ahead and prepares to meet them, but a foolish man goes ahead anyway and is punished."* What is this saying to us today? If you are able to see something is a possibility, you should create a plan to address it before it happens, and if you don't, you are a foolish person. Without an emergency plan, when the unexpected arises, you are forced to incur new debt, pay bills late or potentially go into a deep depression because all of your creditors are calling you.

This is how you create the plan. Don't plan for the *specific event;* instead plan for a *specific amount*. Have a plan for a $250 expense, a

$500 expense or a $1,000 expense and practice the plan regularly. Your written plan should work like this...

*If a $250 expense arose, consider the following (specific steps)

* Reduce meats and deserts - $50
* Eliminate dry cleaners - $50
* Reduce date night for the month - $100
* Skip getting my hair done for a week - $50

* If a $500 expense arose, consider the following (specific steps)

* Reduce meats and deserts - $50
* Eliminate dry cleaners - $50
* Reduce date night for the month - $100
* Skip getting my hair done for a week - $50
* Request overtime for one month $310

* If a $1,000 expense arose, consider the following (specific steps)

* Reduce meats and deserts - $52
* Eliminate dry cleaners - $50
* Reduce date night for the month - $100
* Skip getting my hair done for a week - $50
* Request overtime for one month - $310
* Borrow money from my savings - $200
* Request a deferment on credit cards - $350

The specific event doesn't matter. Focus on a specific amount that allows you to address any event. Practice these plans once a year to make sure they properly work. Money created while practicing the plan can be used to save or even take a vacation. During "A date with your future" spend time looking down the road for potential problems and preparing for them now.

Principle 12 - Run your personal finances
like a highly successful business.

If your company ran their finances as you run your personal finances, how long would you have a job? Why should you manage your money or run your personal finances any differently than a business does? They have spent millions on systems and consultants to ensure they manage their money the best way possible to obtain maximum profits. Why not strive to do the same without needing to spend major resources on systems? What do successful businesses do that you need to do to be successful with your personal finances?

* Create spending plans - They know month by month what their projected income and expenses are and work very hard to stay within their budgeted numbers.

* Review results – Monthly, they review their actual spending against their plan. Any differences initiate corrective actions to get themselves back in line with their spending plan.

* Regular meeting – Meetings are scheduled to enhance the bottom line through cost reduction and creating new sources of income.

* Hire consultants - Assists them in developing strategies to improve profits.

* Mission statement - All of their actions are in line with their mission. In your personal finances I call this *Purpose Spending*. All of your spending should assist in fulfilling your purpose or goals.
* Have a team- The Board of Directors (Financial Empowerment Team) meet on a regular basis to harvest ideas that can make the company more successful.

Chapter 10
Financial Mindsets

You don't need to have a background in finance to do this. All you need is to have a change in mindset to understand these types of items are necessary if you are going to be successful in life.

Principle 13 - Your life will not change until your thinking changes.

People want change in their lives but they don't want to change the right things that will create change. They will change their jobs, the city they live in, image or their spouse and still life does not change significantly. In order for your life to change, you must change your thinking. It's your thinking that creates limitations in your life. It's your thinking that causes you to quit when things get tough. It's your thinking that allows fear to remain in you to keep you from doing what you really need or want to do. It's your thinking that tells you that you can't have more out of life or that you don't deserve better!

This is what your thinking is doing to you, not what others are thinking of you. Your mind can be your greatest asset or your greatest liability. The brain is one of the most powerful organs in your body. It needs instruction in order to function in its designed purpose.

How do you begin changing how you think? Change what you say or believe about yourself, change what you read, change your closest friends and change what you watch on TV. Meditating on these new things will begin to clear out the trash presently in your mind.

Changing your thinking will permanently change your life. Below is the four-step process:
* **Review** - Review what you believe about money; face it to fix it.
* **Remove** - Remove those thoughts that make you poor and compare them to principles in this book.

* Replace - Replace old thoughts with new principles in this book.
* Realign - Realign or get all of your actions to follow the new principles.

Principle 14 - Cash flow is the seed that creates your future.

The most powerful financial concept in the world is cash flow, and it is a word misunderstood by the masses. Many people understand and embrace income but never realize it's not income that should determine the quality of their life; it's cash flow. Income may qualify you for a home but it is cash flow that will allow you to keep the home. Income may allow you to get the newest car but cash flow will allow you to keep that car regardless of economic times. Your cash flow determines the future you create and the quality of your life, how quickly you eliminate debt and increase your credit scores, when and where you go on vacation and how quickly you will acquire assets on sale and become financially free.

It is your cash flow that creates and determines the type future you are creating for your family. Income qualifies you for debt but cash flow eliminates debt.

Principle 15 - People are so busy trying to make
a living they never learn how to make a fortune.

Years ago I remember seeing a cartoon where this man was in his house frantically mopping up the water from his flooded home. Then in the corner of the cartoon there is a little mouse that says, "Why is he so busy mopping up the water. Why not just turn off the faucet?" This cartoon summarizes why people's lives lack change. Though they are doing things, it's not the right things to fix the problem. They are going to work, trying to start a business, requesting overtime but they haven't identified their major problem(s) and work on them.

Is it that we are afraid to face them? Is it that we don't know what they are? Or could it be that we allow ourselves to get busy just to avoid the mess we have created?

People believe the solution to their problems is to work, get a part-time job and make more money. NO! When people do this, they spend more money thus creating more frustration. What if they took that same amount of time and worked on learning about money, then doing what they learned? The solution is to take time to learn how to make a fortune. What are you learning to make this fortune (A date with your future)?

To get free financially you must first free up time. You need time to work on your present so you don't carry the difficulties into your future. You need time to solve your problems, locate solutions, reconcile the bank account and increase your belief about yourself. Busyness keeps you doing without thinking. This tires you out and when you have free time all you desire to do is sleep or watch TV. Stop being so busy and begin to work on your future right now.

Principle 16 - Never allow debt to enter your life until you have clearly marked its exit.

Debt loves to hang around and be a part of your life. It has multiple strategies to begin as a 5-year term but stays for 20 years. Look at your 30-year mortgage that has now grown to over 40 years due to loan modifications, refinances, and late payments. Before you incur any debt, create a written plan outlining exactly how you will pay it off quickly. Here's an example of how I will use this principle to eliminate a 30-year mortgage.

Action	Years
Present Term	30
Draft payment every 2 weeks (half of the regular payment)	20
Pay an extra $50 every two weeks	15
Enhance credit scores to lower the interest rate	12
Allocate half of all raises and business profits to attack debt	9

At the closing table you will obtain a 30-year mortgage but before you sign the papers, you and your spouse should create this plan to pay off this home in 9 years. With this plan, you have clearly marked debts exit before you allowed it to enter your life.

Principle 17 - Your job should be your initial source of money not your permanent source of money.

One of the biggest financial mistakes people make that cause them to spend their entire lives struggling financially is that they never understand the purpose of their job. A famous author once stated, *"When the purpose of a thing is not known abuse is inevitable."* We abuse the purpose of our jobs because we never learn the purpose of them. People believe the primary or major purpose of their job is to pay bills – wrong. The primary purpose of your job is to buy assets on sale. Your assets are designed to pay your bills and buy your luxuries.

The job is the initial source of income while you are learning how to acquire assets on sale. As you learn about different assets like real estate, paper assets, businesses and intellectual properties, you become less and less dependent on your salary.

Question: Are you just as dependent on your salary today as you were when you first began working? If so, you have never learned the purpose of your job and all these years you have been abusing the money you have earned. Over time, you should become less and less dependent on your job and more dependent on your assets.

*Principle 18 - Whenever you waste
money you waste a part of your life.*

If you were doing something you know is causing you to lose or waste part of your life, would you stop it? If each time you did a particular thing you lost 4 hours of your life would this motivate you to change your behavior? Each month, millions of people waste a part of their lives without ever realizing it. When does this happen? It happens when we don't understand the purpose.

Every time you waste money you waste a part of your life. Repeat the previous sentence over again until you feel the pain of the statement. Let's see how much of your life you waste whenever you mismanage or spend meaningless money. I will assume you earn $15 per hour or $31,000 a year.

How Money Is Spent And Wasted	Amount Spent Or Wasted Divided By 15	Amount Of Life Wasted
NSF	$30 / 15	2 hours
Late Fees	$75 / 15	5 hours
Over The Limit Credit Fees	$40 / 15	2 1/2 hours
Interest On Car Loan	$1,500 / 15	100 hours per year
Interest On Home Loan	$8,000 / 15	533 hours per year
A Meal Out	$50 / 15	3.3 hours
Clothing	$200 / 15	13.3 hours

Once you see and better understand this, it should encourage you to better manage your money and stop wasting your life. Before spending money, ask yourself, "Is this the best way to spend my life?"

Principle #19 - Your children should begin where you end.

In the book of Proverbs, chapter 19 and verse 14 says, "House and riches are the inheritance of fathers. . ." What is this saying to us today? It's saying for each child you have, you should leave them, **before you die,** a house and some money.

People of Jewish faith and culture are some of the richest people in the world because this is how they think. Back in biblical times, an inheritance was due to a child and for a parent to be considered a good parent, they had to provide an inheritance. This inheritance was made available for the child even while the parent was alive so the parent could assist the child in multiplying it so that he too could pass it on to his children and their children.

What did your parents leave you? If your parents were like most, they left you nothing financially so you started from where they started; at ground zero. Please don't do to your children what your parents did to you. Your children should begin financially where you ended. You are teaching your children how to manage money so when they receive your assets they understand they are to enjoy them while they are alive and multiply them so that more is passed on to their children.

You see, like a relay race, where you stopped, your children should start which provides them and all subsequent generations a strong foundation to build upon. What if your parents had done this for you - how much better would your life be?

Principle 20 - Financial success is not based on what you make. It's based on how much of what you make you keep.

People attempt to measure your financial success by asking, "Where do you live?" "What do you do for a living?" or "How much do you make?" The more appropriate question should be "How much of what you make do you keep versus give to your creditors?" Has anyone ever asked you that question? If you like your family better than you like your creditors, why are you giving them most of your money? Are you tired of this yet? What you make never produces success. It is what you make and keep that will.

Principle 21 - Never take a job for what you can earn; take it for what you can learn. What you learn will impact what you earn.

The basis for taking a job should be based on what you can learn, what you will be exposed to and who will be teaching you. Again, I look at Jewish people for wisdom. They teach their children to excel in school so they can get the best jobs after graduation. Not to make the most money, but to work with and be trained by the best minds in the world so they will learn how to successfully run and build their own businesses.

What's the message most parents send to their children: "Go to school to get a good job!" If we change the message or understand the purpose of our jobs and that is to learn (you are being paid by your job to learn), what you learn on that job within time will impact what you will earn. Whether you stay with that company for promotions or start your own business, the education you receive will be a determining factor in what you earn.

Principle 22 - You will never control your
money until you first learn to control your life.

I read something once that really gave me a great perspective about managing life. It stated, *"Our days are like identical suitcases, but most people pack more into them than others. That's because they know what to pack."*

All of us receive 24 hours in a day but not everyone gets the same return on his or her 24 hours. The truth is, if you don't manage your time, you can't manage your life. Time cannot be controlled. It marches on no matter what you do. People talk about trying to "find time" but they should quit looking; there isn't any extra lying around. Twenty-four hours is the best any of us are going to get. Successful people understand time is their greatest asset so they protect and guard it. They consistently ask themselves, "Am I getting the best use out of my time?"

Principle 23 - Poverty is a disease of the mind.

There is a very contagious disease in our world today and people don't even know it exists. Most people don't even know they have it but it is the number one killer in the world. It's the number one killer of dreams, potential and therefore lives. This disease is called poverty of the mind. The disease "poverty of the mind" has very little to do with its cousin poverty (not a disease) which says "I don't have anything **now**", but poverty of the mind says, "I don't want any more out of life, I don't believe I can have any more in life or I don't think I deserve any more in life." This disease effects your:

* **Vision** - you don't see your life changing.
* **Energy** - you don't want to do anything to change your life.
* **Speech** - your words are all about what you can't do or have.
* **Dreams** - you don't have any.
* **Relationships** - you only want to be around people who have the disease because they wouldn't challenge you to do more with your potential.

The worse part about this disease is that you pass it on to those that are closest to you like your spouse, children and your friends. There are millions of groups of people in churches, clubs, and companies that have infected one another without anyone being aware. Any time one of the infected members attempts to find a cure for the disease, because they are tired (it takes your energy), the infected members begin to re-infect them again, eliminating their desire to become free. The disease does have cures and here are three of them:

* **Mentorship** - obtain a mentor who will stretch you and who cares more about your future than your feelings.
* **Friends** - who want more out of life and will push you.
* **Education** - invest in your informal education with books, audios and seminars. Life is so much better without this disease.

Principle 24 - Every decision you make, you should make with your future in mind.

Imagine you are about to make a decision on a major purchase. What are the criteria you follow in making this decision? Most people will decide to obtain it if it makes them happy now (immediate gratification), the banks approves the loan, they can afford the monthly payments or it's the latest trend that everyone else has.

By following this process you *fill up our present while robbing your future.* You must begin to think generationally and this requires overcoming selfishness. We should ask ourselves, "How will the decisions I make today impact my family's future?" Below is an example of typical decisions and their impact on our lives:

Item Purchased	Length Of Impact	Benefits
Car	3-5 years	Family enjoy it now
Clothes	2-4 years	You enjoy it now
Sneakers	Less than six months	You enjoy it now
Wide Screen TV	2-4 years	Family enjoy it now
Quality Stocks	10 plus years	You earn dividends and can rent it out to make $
Business with systems	10 plus years	Cash flow for now and for future generations and potentially internationally
Real Estate	10 plus years	Cash flow, tax benefits and ability to create new assets

Principle 25 - Success does not require a job but it does require work.

Whenever someone says, "If you want anything out of life you must work to get it." What comes to mind? Go ahead say it —a job! We have been conditioned to believe the only type of work there is to make money to be successful is working a job. I love what Henry Ford said, *"Thinking is the hardest job that's why so few people do it."* A job is possibly the hardest way to become successful and the numbers support this. Consider two power stats:

1. 95% of the world's population controls 5% of the wealth. What does the 95% of people have in common? They all have a job or own a job because they are self-employed.
2. 90% + of people who work a job at the age of 65, after working 40 years will still need some type of financial support from the government or their families and still need to work.

Here is another point you should consider which will allow you to begin to understand that to be successful does require work but not a job. Robert Kiyosaki stated in *Rich Dad Poor Dad*, *"My friends look for work. I look for assets."* Are you looking for work or assets? Both of these are hard work with major differences.

The Job - It is hard work all your life and becomes harder as you get older. What you will make is limited based on what you do and the company's profits. The income increase is linear and predictable and the source is unstable and subject to many factors that results in job loss.

The Assets - It begins as hard work and over time becomes easier because your systems and your networks bring assets or deals to you. You do the work one time and the money continues to increases over time. The income is exponential and the assets are reliable.

Use the job as the seed that allows you to purchase assets on sale so you can work hard for a shorter period of time with greater results.

Chapter 11
Let Go And Get Moving

You will never change that which you can tolerate or have grown to accept. Whenever someone constantly complains about a situation but never does anything to fix it, it's because it does not hurt bad enough.

The story is told by Les Brown of two friends talking. One of the men has a dog that just continues to howl during the entire conversation. Finally, the friend asks, "What's wrong with your dog?" The dog owner replied, "He is sitting on a nail."

The friend replies, "What? Sitting on a nail? Why doesn't he get up and move?" The owner replied "I guess it doesn't hurt him bad enough."

This is how 95% of people live their lives. They complain about their job, business, finances, weight and life and do nothing about. What are you presently complaining about but have done nothing? Though people complain about various parts of their lives, the reality is it just does not hurt enough. They have grown to accept it because it's all they have known and all their friends have the same complaint so it can't be that bad. Without pain there is no change.

The greatest idea you will ever have in your life, you have not discovered it yet. This is great news that should cause you to be excited each day. This idea awaits your arrival and will provide you with the complete fulfillment you long for. When you develop this mindset, it creates an excitement that motivates you to want to think to discover that most treasured idea.

There are many things in life that are more valuable than money. One of those many things are ideas that have been harvested and turned into an asset. Money, once it is spent is gone forever, however an idea that has been turned into an asset creates money forever.

People have acquired the habit of working for money but have never learned the habit of thinking to create wealth. Thinking allows you to discover ideas that will keep you energized and motivated.

It's Never Too Late

I've learned every problem has multiple solutions. There have been many days where this principle has pulled me out of bed to pursue my dreams another day just after having a devastating defeat hours earlier. It would have been easy to stay in bed wounded, hurt and crushed; making excuses for why my dream would never become a reality.

With the defeat came problems I had yet to solve but I kept telling myself, "EVERY PROBLEM HAS A SOLUTION!" This simple statement was so believed by me that it reawakened and reactivated the giant and greatness on the inside. Just because you may not know the solution does not mean it doesn't exist. We fail to understand there is a difference between a problem and a fact of life.

Facts of life are things that cannot be changed like who your parents are, where you were born and the time or place you were born. Problems all have solutions (job layoff, excessive debt, business won't grow, or poor credit). If you don't have the solutions, find the person who does.

You were born to impact the lives of others. Your success and your ability to overcome adversity must inspire others to do the same. People want to hear a story of triumph that sounds a lot like their own. When you look in the mirror you must not only see your destiny, you must also see the destiny of others tied to what you do.

Remember, from day one, two plans were already established for Simba. There was a plan of destiny and purpose and there was a plan of adversity and death. Similar to Simba, the enemy saw the greatness on the inside of you from the beginning and his job is to hinder you from reaching your purpose.

If you lose focus, life will give you another opportunity in a split second if you (or someone else) remind yourself of the greatness you have within and you tap into The Source. Simba had Nala to remind him of his greatness and the Father as his source.

If you are at rock bottom there's a solution. You may think rock bottom is a bad place, but is it? Granite and lime are two of the most precious stones on earth. However, to get to them you have to dig up some dirt and go through a number of obstacles. Yet when you reach your goal, the circumstances you endured far outweigh the setbacks. Just remember, it's never too late to BECOME what you should have BEEN! Just *Make the Shift* and 'make a date with your future' so you can achieve everything God has purposed in your heart to achieve.

Insightful Reminders

Imagination helps us visit our future so we are motivated to leave our present. God gave us an imagination so that we could see what He sees. Imagination is the ability to allow your mind to run wild so that it can create your future. If you knew you could accomplish your dreams one year from now, would that motivate you? Would it matter what you had to go through to get to your promise?

Seeing what God has promised you and developing a specific plan provides you with motivation to get to your future. Your imagination allows you to visit or see your future, but your well-defined plan takes you to it. Visualize the power of discipline, goals, vision and their affect on your destiny. This will motivate you to leave your present and move towards your future. Your past can't motivate you to leave your present; it created it. You don't have a future when you take your past beyond your present because your present will overtake your future.

Your imagination helps you to see what God sees and destroys depression. Who could get depressed by seeing the same destiny God sees for you? You gain momentum by focusing on where you're going. By setting things such as excessive television, commercials, friends (the ones who lie about your ability) and past failures before you, you program yourself to accept your current position in life. However, you should view your future as a clean sheet of paper; it's spotless. Use your imagination to help take you to your God ordained destiny.

Where Do You Live?

People live in one of three places: hell (not enough), earth (just enough), and heavenly places (more than enough). Having vision involves having well-defined goals and a well-defined plan of action to achieve them. Clearly seeing what you want and how to obtain it gives you motivation to go for it. Where there is no vision, there is no passion or fuel for persistence. Vision is a master plan for achievements and controls every aspect of your life; it's your roadmap for life. Without vision you become lost, frustrated and confused. When you see the same things over and over again, it's a sign that you are lost and need some direction in your life. Not having vision is like riding in a car to a place you've never been before with no map and no directions. It takes longer to get to your destination (if you arrive there at all) and you must constantly stop to assess where you are. You become more vulnerable to unexpected dangers and incidents and lose motivation to press toward your destination.

How many times have people become lost trying to find a destination, given up and went back to where they came from? With a vision, you've visited your final destination many times before in your mind and you know it's worth the journey. Vision provides you constant abundance while you wait for your reward.

The absence of vision leaves you living in personal and financial hell and prevents you from sitting in heavenly places on earth. Vision from God never comes with rear view mirrors. Your vision should fill you so much that though you see things you like (cars, homes, clothing, etc.), you are filled and satisfied with your vision and you have no more room in your life for anything outside of becoming more than what you are.

You Must See Big Things

Have a vision that stretches you and requires God to obtain it. You now have the persistence to push through obstacles and delays. You have to see your end before the beginning and though others abandoned or scaled down their vision, you are pressing to obtain yours.

It's impossible for a double-minded man to make a stable decision. Until you decide what you want in and out of life, your life will be unstable. You have what it takes on the inside of you to become more than ordinary. Goals are your anchors that keep you from being swept away by the winds of negative people, negative thoughts and overspending; goals keep you from going to extremes.

Always remember, you must believe you are more than what you have become and it's never too late to remember you are the heir to the throne. Feeding into past failures creates a lack of motivation and stability and instability is a breeding ground for frustration.

Many people change their minds based on the obstacles thrown before them. Obstacles are designed to change your direction, but not your final destination. Without a clear destination, you won't be prepared when a big opportunity arises. Begin to believe you deserve to be more in life as you also begin to let go of your past and those who don't believe. Before there can be success, there first must be stability.

Most People Adopt A Dream Rather Than Conceive A Vision

The dream most people adopt is called the "American Dream." It says to purchase a home with a 30-year mortgage, buy 2 cars, embrace a working wife, factor her income into the family budget, and then retire at 65. Because this is the American lifestyle, we accept it. However, I believe YOU can do better. Everyone from family and friends, to the media and Internet encourages us to live this way. By doing this, you are living someone else's dream that has limited vision. You must understand there is more to life. Your vision should stretch you.

You'll know when you've moved from adopting a dream to conceiving a vision when it requires something greater and you're left with more than enough to help others. The American dream contains just enough for you and your family, so it can't be enough for your vision.

True vision requires you to decide what you want, not what others say you should have. Visions are conceived; dreams are adopted. Conception takes time to develop and a tolerance for pain. With childbirth, the pain is over within hours, with a vision it's for life. There must be intimate time alone with your vision (natural conception takes seconds but conceiving a vision requires days and months alone with God) and the help of others to deliver (mentors and counselors) and care for the child (vision). What is conceived resembles the parents, what is adopted resembles someone else. People who haven't conceived a vision often say they wish they were doing something different. Why? Because what they are currently doing really isn't on the inside of them waiting to be birthed. WARNING: Visions, like newborn babies, are very fragile; require proper handling, nurturing and care to be sustained. If not, they ultimately die!

Faithfulness Is Simply Faith In Its Fullness

The level of faith you have in your goals and visions will determine how faithful you are to them. Faith is simply being persuaded that the object of your faith will meet your expectations. When you believe, you are faithful to that object. Regardless of the setbacks, you see them only as temporary obstacles to a permanent end. People who are not faithful to their dreams, goals and visions obviously don't believe it will work. If they saw their dreams, goals and visions taking them where they desired to go, they would stick with it to get there.

The same faithfulness required to have a successful relationship is also needed to have a successful legacy. You must be willing to believe in yourself and stick with your plan until you obtain the desired results. Don't be distracted by others' actions and opinions. The only people that should make a difference in your decisions are those that have been where you are trying to go, and those who are willing to help you get there.

Champions Are Never Remembered By How They Started

People are great starters when it is something new and everybody else wants to do it. Many times, after the excitement of the moment has calmed, it is typical to assess that people start things but don't finish.

Either they didn't count the cost, didn't have a plan, or they lost motivation. No matter how well you start, you never qualify for rewards unless you finish. You must learn to become a finisher in a world of starters.

When a baseball professional gets to third base but fails to score, he does nothing for the team and is considered a "standard base runner." Many people have standard dreams. They have come so close to scoring but their rally falls short because they don't believe they can achieve the goal. They think it can happen for others but not for them, therefore, they lose motivation or they fail and never try again.

We forget the failures of great people and only record in history their successes. In their failure, they found a seed of success that motivated them to finish the race and receive their crown. Getting started is progress but finishing is success. Can you name one thing in life that yields the same results for those who start versus those who finish? NO!! The prize is only given to those who are fearless to begin and courageous enough to finish.

Obstacles Should Change Your Direction, Not Your Destination

Unexpected events are a fact of life and cannot be avoided. Proverbs 22:3 describes it this way: "*A prudent man foresees the difficulties ahead and prepares for them; the simpleton goes blindly on and suffers the consequences.*" It is wise to plan alternate routes to accomplish your dreams and goals, but never alter your destination. Be flexible enough to change your plans to deal with adversity or even new information.

Detours are designed to take you to the same place, while using a different route. People who are sidetracked by adversity usually end up failing. View every adversity as an opportunity to find a creative way to do something. That same creative way may be efficient when there is no adversity. It is through creative thinking that great ideas are born. Successful people always ask themselves, "How can I do what I'm currently doing better?" Even after you set a plan to do something, challenge it.

Successful people believe nothing that exists is in its perfected state. While you can't choose your circumstances, you can choose your thoughts, and thoughts determine actions. Keep in mind, people don't drown by falling in water, instead, they drown by staying in it. View obstacles as blessings that keep you from arriving at your destination before you are ready to handle it.

Never confuse a delay with a failure; delays are not denials. If you believe in yourself and have a passion for your dream, you should see delays as fuel to reach your destination. Get with your Financial Empowerment Team, spouse, or covenant partner(s) to discuss ways to overcome your obstacles. Most people see an obstacle as an ending point, but successful people see an obstacle as a turning point.

The Power In Your Belief

If you are passionate about your goals and dreams, your belief in them is no more powerful than the actions you put with them. What actions are you taking to make your dreams and goals come to pass? If one of your dreams and goals is to become a millionaire, do you read, study and save like a millionaire?

Belief and faith is based on consistency, not deeds. Actions are what gives your belief and faith life and distinguishes your belief and faith in yourself from the belief and faith of others. Without actions, your belief and faith in yourself, your dreams and your success is impossible. Regardless of how much you believe for something to happen, without action, it will not come to pass. Think of it this way: Cement can't fulfill its full potential until it is first mixed with water. Likewise, your belief and faith in yourself cannot reach its full potential without action.

As previously stated throughout this book, having faith and believing in yourself gives you vision. Without vision, there is no passion, and passion is your fuel for persistence. Most people want instant gratification, therefore, when goals are not met quickly, the goals are quickly scaled down or abandoned. If you stop before you obtain your desired result that simply means you didn't believe you could have it before you started.

To be in agreement and succeed with something greater than you (visions and goals), your faith and your works must be at the same level. When you start listening to those who say you can't achieve your dreams, listen to those who provide negative thoughts about your dreams or abandon your written goals that area of your belief and faith has just died.

The harder you work for something, the more you believe you deserve to have it. The road to success is a marathon, not a sprint. You must master the discipline of persistence. Start today by mixing your belief and faith in yourself with the corresponding action. Remember, you are more than what you have become and each step you take in moving forward with your vision guarantees you are one step closer to your dreams.

Marry Your Purpose

Having goals is not enough. You must achieve them in order to have real success. Most people are content with just having goals, but it takes commitment (being married to your goals) in order to give birth to them. Most people don't want to marry their goals; they simply want to date them.

Dating requires no commitment and if things become difficult, you can call it quits and lose nothing. However, when you are married to something, you are committed to fulfilling its purpose, regardless of the cost. When people marry, they vow during marriage to stick through things "for better or for worse" meaning conditions don't determine your commitment.

Success takes faithfulness and dedication. With marriage, there is real intimacy, one common purpose, life-long commitment, quality and constant time together. The marriage to your vision requires the same thing to be successful. You must be willing to ignore distractions and do whatever is necessary to supply all that is needed to have a fulfilling marriage to your vision.

While there is pain in giving birth, the joy of the newborn baby (vision) makes it worthwhile. While people say they want to give birth to their goals, many are afraid and unwilling to make a commitment to them. The birthing not only takes time, it also takes nurturing and caring after the birth or it will die. Just as people want the benefits of marriage (companionship and sex) without commitment, they also want the success of goal setting without the commitment. The same amount of passion you have for loving and being committed to your family, you should have for your vision and goals. Take this very moment to list your goals and write beside each one of them whether you are married to them versus dating them.

Your Own Binoculars

Regardless of how close two people's eyeglass prescriptions may be, you see best using your own glasses. It's the same with seeing your vision and purpose. The only way to have a productive life is to see *your* vision with *your* eyes. Allow your dreams and visions to be your standard for judgment and the controller of your desires. Never be afraid to be different from the crowd.

No one can determine for you what you want out of life. Goals should be based on what's important to you and your family, not the opinions of other people. Each family should adopt internal principles that shape every area of their lives. Whenever you follow someone else's plans, you end up where they wanted to be and not where you wanted to be. By getting other's opinions and insights based on your plan, you gain wisdom and understanding of things to come and ways to become more successful. However, get their insight only to *enhance your vision, not to embrace their vision.* When you focus solely on what others think, you cloud your vision with theirs. When this happens, you see the wrong things and therefore go in the wrong direction. Other people should enhance your vision without causing you to lose focus of it.

Define your dream life then pursue that dream with a passion. Dreams do come true if you wake up and pursue them. Challenge yourself to break the norms of society and live a better life. Who says you must work until 65? Who says you can't pay for your homes and cars with cash? Who says you can't fulfill your dreams and leave a legacy for your grandchildren? Regardless of what others say, what *you* say will determine what you have! Remember, glasses are specifically made based on a person's vision. Therefore, you can't expect your vision to be clear looking through someone else's prescription.

See What Others Don't

While he was a successful entrepreneur, Walt Disney died before the completion of Disney World, yet his vision lives on. After its completion, a reporter mentioned to one of Mr. Disney's team members how it was a shame Mr. Disney didn't live to see his vision come to pass. The response from the team member was that Disney World existed because Mr. Disney saw it in his vision.

Vision is one of the most powerful abilities of mankind. Nothing has ever been done that wasn't first seen by its creator. The way God knew the earth and all its creations were good was by knowing how it should look before it was manifested based on a vision. If vision was important to God's creation, it should be important to ours.

Whatever you are striving for must first be seen before it can be attained. The first step in fulfilling your vision, seeing your dreams come true, believing in yourself, and completing your goals is seeing yourself doing it. Scientific studies show that if you constantly think on or say something with passion, your mind is triggered because it thinks it's a command, not just a thought, and assumes the responsibility for finding ways to make your vision become a reality.

Your body is programmed to respond to vision, therefore, the reason many people don't have what they want is because they haven't given their body anything to respond to. Seeing something to the point that it's real to you requires time alone with your vision to "open your eyes" and see it clearly. Seeing the vision gives you the passion, drive and energy to move forward and attain it. When the process of seeing your vision is complete, now you can attain what you've seen because your mind translated words into pictures. This is why your belief and confessions about your visions and dreams are so important. Your mind sees what you say, giving it a blueprint for success. Even in reading this book, your mind is trying to develop mental images to bring understanding and revelation to the words. Vision is important to your legacy and without it, your dreams are incomplete.

Plan Your Future

Many people spend more time on things that are interesting (planning a vacation) than they do on things that are important (creating a legacy). Consider the amount of time that was spent planning your vacation, wedding, Christmas and home decorations. If the time spent planning these things exceeds the time spent planning and preparing your future, your priorities are out of order.

Each of these events last less than ten days and involves months of planning while your future lasts the rest of your life and is planned in minutes. By regularly reviewing your goals, you know the status of each and are more prepared to control future events. There should be weekly reviews of your goals to prepare for the future and to enhance your vision. If you don't work as hard managing your future as you do making it, you will never reach your full vision and potential. Ladies and gentlemen, it's time that you move forward and begin *Making The Shift*.

Transform Your Life

There are several positive, constructive and psychological, sound productive behaviors you can practice to improve your personal life and the life of your business. To ensure your success in both areas, you must control your life in order to maximize your personal and business development.

The Process - To begin, you must change your environment to change your destiny. A change in your environment forces you to change your mind-set. Your mind-set is simply what you believe to be true about yourself and your future. Train your mind to think positively, to see the invisible, to seek solutions, to create ideas, to see yourself with more and to see into the future believing anything is possible.

As a result, this changes your actions. You begin to daily, have a *Date with Your Future*, systemize your life flow, stop time leaks, embrace fitness and health, maintain proper rest and create written plans of action to follow each day; moving you closer to fulfilling your life's purpose. Through this process, the invisible becomes visible. Remember, everything that's seen was made by things that are unseen. Your ideas, beliefs and plans are unseen things that, when combined with action, produces the life you desire.

Environment - You will conform to or become a product of your environment. You must create and live in an environment that helps you believe that being more, having more and doing more is available and attainable.

Evaluate some of the things in your environment. Look at your friends, your relationships, where you live, television, music, what you read, the places you travel the seminars you attend, mentors you implore; the dreams and goals you passionately and consistently think about, and what you say about yourself and your own situation.

To begin changing your environment in order to improve and achieve your goals, start by being around or talking to people who are successful while eliminating your time with people who are negative and lack passion. In addition, begin reading books and attending webinars or seminars of people who are successful in your area of interest to implement a portion of their techniques on success and achievement.

The benefits of embracing change in your environment are tremendous. A new environment causes you to dream bigger, remove limitations and births in you the belief that anything is possible. As a result, your mind is expanded to know that more is available and not only do you begin to want to achieve more; you begin believing you can accomplish more. In this environment, you begin seeing your potential and you realize, if they can do it, I'm no different and I can do it too.

Relationships - Look at your friends and relationships and decide if they are assets or liabilities. Assets are those who are actively helping you to reach your goals and dreams. *Critical Reminder*: Liabilities are those who "lie about your ability" by telling you that you can't do it. GET RID OF ALL LIABILITIES!!

Who do you have active in your life that has the ability to stretch you to reach your potential? What relationships do you have that can stretch your business and move to the next level? The right friends, books, mentors and business associates can move to exponentially achieve dreams you didn't think were possible.

Mindset - There are two systems that impact mindset. Those systems are an impoverishing system and an empowering system. Both systems are competing with one another, so you must learn to fight against the impoverishing system, while embracing the empowering system. The best way to accomplish this task is to think more positive thoughts and to embrace a new environment that is full of life, passion, success and productivity. Remember, the environment you choose to live in or expose yourself to, impacts your mind the most.

Acknowledgements

I am grateful to God for entrusting me to serve His people in a way that will uplift them and empower them for living an amazing life and having a business with Him as the central focus.

Special thanks, honor, and respect to my parents for helping me to become the man I am today and for raising me within a home that honored Christ. You have inspired me more than you'll ever know. Your inspiration helped me to think bigger and beyond what I thought was possible! Thank you for your love.

I want to thank my sisters for continuously listening to my ideas, thoughts and insight. Your love is truly amazing.

A special thanks to my business partner who always believes in me, supports me and encourages me. Thanks for your patience and for giving me space to pursue my dreams and passion. Thank you for your friendship and being a caring and understanding individual. You've made this an awesome process! I am so grateful God saw fit for our paths to cross. I look forward to what God will do through us as we continue on this assignment!

And to my family and friends (regretfully I can't mention you all), thank you so much for your prayers, love, and continued support. I love you and appreciate you!

About The Author

Vincent K. Harris has launched multiple successful brands in the non-profit and business arena that assists others in pursuing their passion and getting results in their lives to create a generational legacy. He regularly speaks and consults with Business Owners, Entrepreneurs, Leaders and Creatives about success in life, business, marketing and content creation. As a Peak Performance Strategist, Vincent's goal is to add more value to your life than you ever dreamed possible by giving you and your organization the tools you can use immediately to improve your community, business and life.

He's here to help you build a legacy, not just a name. The legacy he's talking about reaches far beyond money and toys. A legacy means having an impact in your business, personal life, community and generations from now, using your amazing talents and abilities to change the world.

If you're like him, you prefer not to live in a box. In fact, you probably destroyed the box to keep it from limiting your thinking a long time ago. He's a business strategist, marketing connoisseur and speaker with a side dish of smiles and laughter. As a southern gentleman from North Carolina with nothing more than a passion, dream and vision, he created a mindset and business that resonates with thought-leaders and community leaders in a powerful way. He helps people dream big and back it up with daily actions to create measurable results.

Get Connected! Connect with across social media:

VinceHarrisSpeaks.com
VinceOnBusiness.com
Twitter: @VinceOnBusiness
Facebook: @VinceOnBusiness
YouTube: @VinceOnBusiness
YouTube: @VinceHarrisSpeaks

www.ingramcontent.com/pod-product-compliance
Lightning Source LLC
Chambersburg PA
CBHW071243170526
45165CB00003B/1221